FRIESLAND
1711
Sneek
IJlst
Heerenveen
Slooten
Winschoten
Wedde
Westerwolde
1722
Steenwijk
Ruinen
Hoogeveen
Meppel
Coevorden
Schokland
Urk
Vollenhove
Vecht
Hasselt
Ommen
Hardenberg
KAMPEN
ZWOLLE
BENTHEIM
OVERIJSSEL
1747
Hattem
Elburg
Almelo
Oldenzaal
Harderwijk
DEVENTER
Goor
BENTHEIM
Apeldoorn
IJssel
Enschede
ZUTPHEN
1722
Lochem
Borculo
Wijk by Duurstede
Rhenen
Wageningen
ARNHEM
Doesborgh
Groenlo
Doetinchem
Bredevoort

Claartje Lindhout

PREFACE

Except for carrying a very Dutch name and working in the kitchen, I actually knew barely anything about Dutch cuisine. Yes, I knew mashed vegetables ('stamppot'), croquettes and potatoes – but that was about it.

What a shame it is that the knowledge of Dutch cooking has almost disappeared in our multicultural society. It is time, I thought, to find out more about my own culinary heritage.

I found out soon enough that each Dutch province had certain specific traditional dishes that have been made there for years and years, and are still being made. Except for Flevoland of course, since that is quite a young province. I chose to compose a mini menu for each province to introduce you to these typical regional dishes.

This book, *The Dutch Kitchen*, contains many easy to make, filling dishes that are based on simplicity and frugalness. If you don't appreciate the small things, you're not worthy of the big ones – as an old Dutch saying goes!

There are several well-known classics in this book, but you will also be surprised by some 'forgotten' dishes. And although I stayed true to the original recipes, I did adjust them slightly here and there. And with that, I mainly mean the quantities – because those were enormous! These are absolutely no luxurious dishes, but they've come straight from the farming countryside. So they're simple, they're cheap and they taste good, because that is what it is all about.

I hope this book will inspire you to try those really traditional regional dishes, like 'Jan-in-de-zak' (Jack-in-the-bag). But also remember: don't rush and take your time!

The DUTCH KITCHEN

Claartje Lindhout

Photography RENE MESMAN *Styling* HANNA VAN DEN BOS
Design & illustrations FLEUR VAN MAARSCHALKERWAART

BECHT

Contents

Contents

Introduction

THE DUTCH KITCHEN

As I said earlier, Dutch cuisine was pretty much unknown to me. But I could say that now I'm rather aware of my culinary heritage. I undertook a delicious quest to the roots and backgrounds of it for this book about the Dutch cuisine.

The quest started – could it be otherwise? – with my mother and grandmother. They gave me cookery books with notes in them and loose pages. Reading and especially cooking from these books, made that I felt a little more close to them, and in that way to my own history as well.

Our society has become one big melting pot of different cultures, something one also notices when looking at the food we eat. Take spices like cloves, cinnamon, ginger and vanilla: these came from the Dutch East Indies and we can't do without them anymore. They are a great contribution to our cooking but our own cuisine seems to get pushed to the background a bit and that would be an awful shame.

From my quest I learned that our cuisine is actually a real honest, purely organic and sustainable way of cooking. This is no kitchen for people that are in a hurry. Nothing gets wasted, you use seasonal and locally grown produce. Real slow food*, actually!

And so it is time to proudly put the balkenbrij back on the table. Balkenbrij was a dish that came from poverty. It is a kind of porridge made with meat left overs. But with my minor changes the balkenbrij has turned into a tasty terrine. It is a dish to surprise guests with – and there's a nice story to be told about it too. Besides, it's not an expensive dish, which is also important in these times.

But what exactly *is* Dutch cuisine? Let the recipes tell you the answer. I hope you will have lots of fun and I wish you good luck with preparing these Dutch dishes!

Note: Because Flevoland hasn't existed for a very long time (it is a province built on reclaimed land) and therefore doesn't have any traditional regional dishes, the Flevoland menu is based on different choices. I chose pancakes (because people often say Flevoland is as flat as one) with elderflower syrup (because elderflower grows there), pheasant (they run around there a lot) with Jerusalem artichoke (which is grown there) and potato cheese croquette (because no Dutch cookery book is complete without a croquette – and potato and cheese are two very Dutch ingredients).

** The slow food movement is a response against the so-called fast food and it hopes to preserve cultural or traditional cuisine. Traditional vegetables, seeds and meats and the agricultural traditions of a certain region are used and being kept alive.*

GOOD TO KNOW

Even though they are based on old recipes, the dishes in this book have to be treated as guidelines. Don't let them stop you leaving things out or adding things in! Personally, I've only adjusted the quantities and added some herbs and spices here and there.
The kind of oven you have (and its temperature) can be different from the one I used. I used a fan assisted oven and the temperatures in this book have been based upon that. But do trust your experience and your own oven! Mine, for instance, has got a hot spot in the back, on the right side…

In this book I use several abbreviations:

tablespoon = tbsp (15 g)
teaspoon = tsp (5 g)
gram = g
kilo = kg
decilitre = dl
centilitre = cl
millilitre = ml

Some kitchen appliances not everyone may own:

meat thermometer
  core temperature
  50–55 °C / 122–131 °F = rare
  60–65 °C / 140–149 °F = medium
  70–75 °C / 158–167 °F = well done
butcher's twine
hand held blender
Kitchen-aid
food processor
cheese cloth
pestle and mortar
baking paper
pâté dish

Groningen menu

PEA SOUP

250 g dried peas	*1 celeriac*
250 g split peas	*4 potatoes (bintje)*
3 onions	*1 smoked sausage*
1 big carrot	*½ bunch of flat leaf parsley*
200 g ham hock	*½ bunch of leaf celery*
250 g smoked bacon	*½ chilli*
1 tbsp fresh thyme, finely chopped	*salt & pepper*
2 fresh bay leaves	*olive oil*
2 small leeks, washed	

serves 6 – 1 night preparation – 2 hours to cook

1. Wash the peas and split peas, put them in a pan, add water untill just above the peas and let them soak for a night.
2. Peel the onions and chop finely.
3. Peel the carrot and dice it.
4. Add the onions, ham hock, bacon, chilli, thyme, bay leaves and salt & pepper to the peas in the soaking water, bring to the boil and stew for 2 hours on low heat.
5. Slice the washed leeks finely. Peel the celeriac and the potatoes and cut them in cubes. Add these to the soup after 2 hours and boil on low heat.
6. Warm up the smoked sausage in hot water on low heat for 15 minutes.
7. Remove the ham hock, bacon, chilli and bay leaves from the soup.
8. Slice the smoked sausage, take the meat off the bone and cut the bacon into cubes. Add all the meat to the soup.
9. Season the soup with the washed and cut flat leaf parsley, leaf celery and salt & pepper.
10. Just before serving, add a swirl of olive oil to the soup.

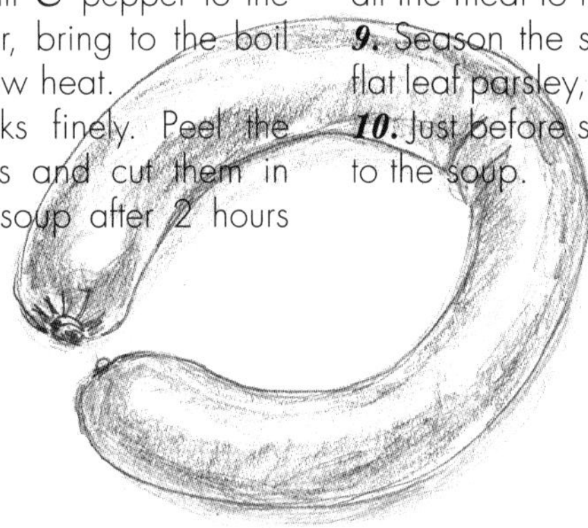

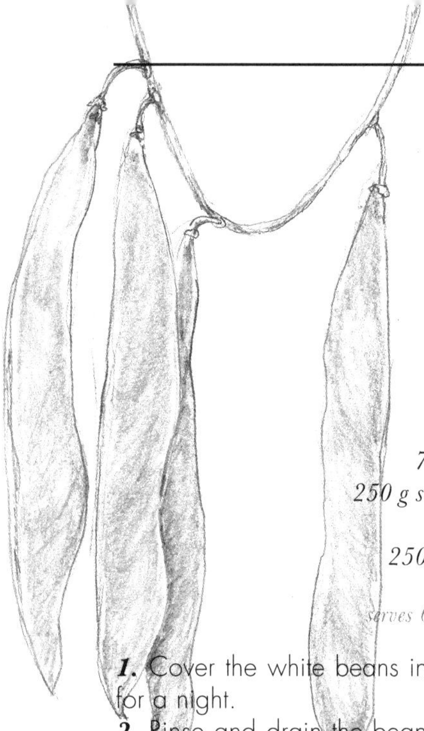

Groningen menu

AUTUMN MASH

750 g floury potatoes	*salt & pepper*
250 g smoked streaky bacon	*100 g butter*
500 g runner beans	*4 tbsp olive oil*
250 g dried white beans	*1 tbsp freshly grated nutmeg*

serves 6 – 1 night preparation – 1 hour and 20 minutes to cook

1. Cover the white beans in water and soak for a night.
2. Rinse and drain the beans, put them back in the pan, cover with plenty water and boil for an hour until done (20 minutes if you have a pressure cooker). Don't add salt or vinegar as this slows down the process.
3. Wash and peel the potatoes and cut them in pieces. Put in a pan with the bacon, cover with water and cook for 20 minutes until done.
4. Put a pan of salted water on high heat and bring to the boil.
5. In the meantime, wash the runner beans and slice them into pieces at an angle. Add to the boiling water and cook for 8 minutes until done.
6. Remove the bacon from the pan and add the runner beans and white beans to the pan with the potatoes. Boil this gently for another 5 minutes.
7. Drain the potatoes, runner beans and white beans and puree them with a masher, together with the butter and olive oil.
8. Add pepper and freshly grated nutmeg to taste.
9. You could dice the left over bacon and stir this through.
10. Just before serving, sprinkle a bit of olive oil over the mash.

Groningen menu

STRAINED YOGURT WITH RHUBARB

300 g yogurt with at least 10% fat content
200 ml whipping cream
3 tbsp icing sugar
zest and juice from 1 lime
1 vanilla pod

RUBARB
200 ml cider
4 stalks of rhubarb
3 tbsp icing sugar
1 tbsp ginger syrup

serves 6 – 1 night preparation – 30 minutes to marinate – 20 minutes to cook

1. Rinse a clean tea towel under the tap to remove any soapy residue.
2. Line a rounded sieve with the tea towel and put it on top of a bowl.
3. Pour the yogurt into the tea towel, close the tea towel with a knot and place something heavy on top. Put in the fridge overnight.
4. Scrape the seeds from the vanilla pod. Grate the zest off the lime, juice it and mix with a fork the zest and juice with the icing sugar and the vanilla seeds.
5. Whip the cream with one tablespoon of icing sugar until it starts to thicken.
6. Whip the strained yogurt and add the lime-vanilla mix.
7. Mix well and fold through the whipped cream. Set aside in the fridge.
8. Wash the rhubarb and dice it finely.
9. Bring the cider just to the boil with the empty vanilla pod, icing sugar and ginger syrup and then turn off the heat.
10. Add the diced rhubarb and leave to stand for at least 30 minutes.
11. Serve the strained yogurt with the marinated rhubarb.
Nice with some thin strips of fresh mint!

Friesland menu

SIPELSOP

(ONION SOUP)

4 eggs	*200 g Frisian cheese with cloves, grated*
500 g onions, diced	*1 tbsp chives, finely chopped*
60 g butter, diced	*1 tsp freshly grated nutmeg*
1 litre chicken or vegetable stock	*salt & pepper*
2 tsp white wine vinegar	

serves 6 – 20 minutes to cook

1. Boil the eggs for 6 minutes until hard boiled.
2. Melt the butter in a big soup pan and fry the onions gently until soft.
3. Add the stock.
4. Bring the soup to the boil and boil gently for 5 minutes.
5. In the meantime, peel the eggs, mash them with a fork and divide the mash over the plates.
6. Season the soup with salt & pepper. Add the nutmeg and stir in the vinegar.
7. Ladle the soup onto the plates and add the grated cheese.
8. Finish with the chives.

Friesland menu

SNORREPOTSJE

(VEAL STEW)

250 g veal
1 veal tongue
1 veal kidney
175 g veal liver
4 banana shallots, cut into half rings
½ chilli
2 cloves
1 tbsp fresh thyme, finely chopped
3 whole mace
2 fresh bay leaves
5 tbsp olive oil
5 tomatoes, diced
2 tbsp red wine vinegar
salt & pepper

serves 6 – 2 hours preparation – 2½ hours to cook

1. Salt all the veal, put the pieces in a big pan of water and leave to stand for 2 hours.
2. Bring to the boil, turn down the heat and stew the meat for at least 1 hour on a low heat. Turn off the heat and leave to cool down.
3. While the meat is cooling down in the liquid, heat the olive oil in a big heavy casserole with thick bottom. Gently fry the shallots until soft.
4. Add the tomatoes, thyme, mace, bay leaf, cloves, chilli and pepper and salt and give it a good stir.
5. Take the meat out of the liquid and dice it (I chose to cut the tongue into long strips to create different textures), then add it to the casserole. Stir well. Add liquid from the other pan until everything is just covered.
6. Stir through the red wine vinegar and bring everything to the boil. Turn down the heat, cover the casserole and leave to stew for another hour. Stir every now and then to prevent the meat from sticking to the bottom of the pan.

Friesland menu

SUGAR BREAD

150 g butter	*6 candied ginger, finely chopped*
500 g flour	*2 eggs*
¼ tsp salt	*2 tsp cinnamon*
1½ dl milk	*½ tsp chilli powder*
35 g fresh yeast	*150 g rock sugar*
4 tbsp ginger syrup	*150 g granulated sugar*

serves 6 – 1 hour and 45 minutes preparation – 30 minutes to cook

1. Heat the milk until lukewarm and stir in the yeast.
2. Sift the flour and salt over a bowl while melting the butter in a small sauce pan on low heat.
3. Make a well in the flour and pour in the yeasty milk, ginger syrup, ginger, melted butter, granulated sugar, chilli and eggs.
4. Knead all this until you've got a nice dough ball.
5. Put the dough ball in the bowl, cover with a damp tea towel and leave in a warm spot to rise for 1½ hour.
6. Then knead in the cinnamon and rock sugar.
7. Grease a bread or cake tin.
8. Put the dough in the tin, cover with the damp tea towel and leave to rise in a warm spot for 25 minutes.
9. Sprinkle the top of the bread with the rock sugar.
10. Put the sugar bread in the preheated oven (200 °C / 392 °F) and leave for 30 minutes. Tip: insert a skewer in the bread – if it comes out clean, the bread is ready.
11. Turn the tin over on top of a cooling rack and leave to cool completely.

Serve this as a dessert: it's lovely to fry thin slices in butter and serve these with cinnamon ice cream. Or make eggy bread: soak the slices of sugar bread in beaten egg and fry them until golden brown on both sides.

Note: I used candied ginger and chilli powder in this recipe, but if you don't like those, you can just leave them out. You could replace the ginger syrup with normal sugar syrup.

Drenthe menu

FARMER'S SALAD WITH BEETROOT AND ORANGES

6 baby beetroots, with leaves
3 tbsp olive oil
1 tbsp mint, finely chopped
1 tbsp chives, finely chopped
2 oranges
1 clove of garlic, finely chopped
1 onion, diced
salt & pepper

serves 4 – 40 minutes preparation – 20 minutes to cook

1. Wash the beetroot leaves and scrub the beetroots under the tap.
2. Cut off the leaves and stems from the beets.
3. Boil the beets in 30 minutes in salted water on high heat.
4. Meanwhile cut the stems finely and tear the leaves to pieces.
5. Fry the stems in 1 tablespoon olive oil in a frying pan for 3 minutes on high heat, then add the onion and garlic. Fry for 5 minutes while stirring constantly.
6. Add the beet leaves and fry along for 1 minute. Add salt & pepper to taste.
7. From one orange, cut away the orange segments from the membranes and put them in a bowl.
8. Add the chives, the mint and the fried beet leaves and stems.
9. Add the juice of the other orange and 2 tbsp olive oil.
10. Take the beets off the heat, rinse with cold water, drain and let them cool down. Cut in segments and add those to the rest of the salad.
11. Mix everything well and add salt & pepper to taste.

Drenthe menu

SIEPELHACHEE

(STEW WITH ONIONS)

10 shallots	*3 slices gingerbread loaf*
750 g lean braising steak	*3 tbsp olive oil*
1 bottle of dark beer or stout	*500 ml vegetable, chicken or beef stock*
½ chilli	*salt & pepper*
2 tbsp fresh thyme, chopped	*50 g butter*
4 cloves	*2 tbsp olive oil*
3 fresh bay leaves (or 5 dried)	

serves 4 – 8 hours preparation – 60 minutes to cook

1. Cut the meat in 2 cm cubes and rub all over with pepper & salt.
2. Pour the beer over the meat and add the bay leaves, chilli, thyme and cloves. Cover and leave in the fridge for at least 8 hours.
3. Cut the slices of gingerbread loaf in cubes.
4. Melt the butter with some olive oil in a casserole with a thick bottom on high heat.
5. Remove the meat from the marinade and dry it with kitchen paper. Fry it in the pan until it is brown on the outsides.
6. Pour the marinade and stock in the casserole and add the pieces of gingerbread loaf. Bring to the boil.
7. Boil for 20 minutes on low heat.
8. In the meantime, peel the shallots, slice them in rings and and add them to the meat. Leave to stew for another 20 minutes until the shallots are done.

Serve with mashed potatoes and red cabbage, for instance.

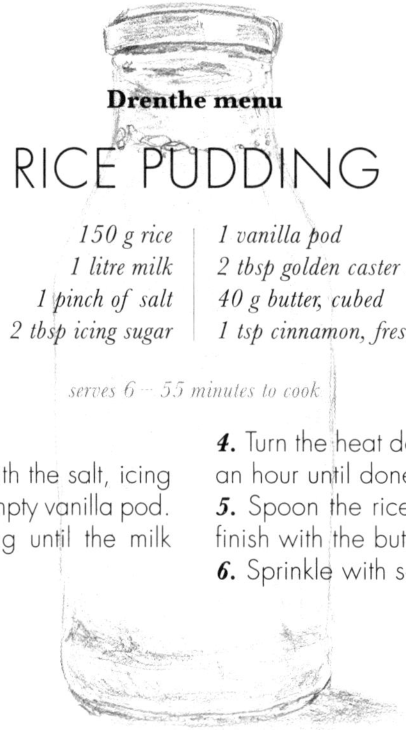

Drenthe menu

RICE PUDDING

150 g rice
1 litre milk
1 pinch of salt
2 tbsp icing sugar
1 vanilla pod
2 tbsp golden caster sugar
40 g butter, cubed
1 tsp cinnamon, freshly grated

serves 6 – 55 minutes to cook

1. Wash and drain the rice.
2. Bring the milk to the boil with the salt, icing sugar, vanilla seeds and the empty vanilla pod.
3. Add the rice. Keep stirring until the milk boils again.
4. Turn the heat down and boil the rice for half an hour until done.
5. Spoon the rice pudding on the plates and finish with the butter and caster sugar.
6. Sprinkle with some cinnamon and serve.

Overijssel menu

BALKENBRIJ (PÂTÉ) WITH SAUERKRAUT

serves 12 – 24 hours preparation – 2 hours to cook

500 g sauerkraut
1 glass of cider
50 g butter
1 fresh bay leaf
1 tsp fresh thyme, finely chopped
salt & pepper

1. Drain the sauerkraut and rinse under the tap.
2. Put the sauerkraut in a sauce pan with the cider, butter, thyme and bay leaf and put it on high heat until boiling.
3. Turn the heat down and leave to boil for 15 minutes. Stir every now and then and season to taste with salt & pepper.

300 g smoked bacon
500 g pig's liver
2 litre chicken, vegetable, mushroom or game stock
3 tbsp fresh thyme, finely chopped
300 g raw pig fat
1½ tsp salt
2 tsp white pepper, freshly ground
1 tsp nutmeg
3 cloves, crushed
750 g buckwheat flour
200 g boiled and smoked streaky bacon, in thin slices
½ tsp chilli powder
1 tbsp lemon zest

1. Dice the smoked bacon and add to a big soup pan with the liver, thyme and stock.
2. Bring to the boil, turn down the heat and let it all stew for 1 hour.
3. In the meantime, dice the pig fat and fry in a frying pan on low heat. This is what the Dutch call 'kaantjes'.
4. Take the liver out of the liquid and puree it in the food processor.
5. Put the liver puree back into the pan and also add the kaantjes and their fat.
6. Add salt, pepper, nutmeg, cloves, chilli powder, lemon zest and the buckwheat flour and stir through.
7. Keep stirring with a wooden spoon until it has reached a thick consistency (the spoon should be able to stand up in it).
8. Leave the pan on the heat for a while until you've heard the air bubbles pop at least five times.
9. Roll out a big piece of cling film on your worktop and lay down the slices of boiled and smoked streaky bacon in a rectangle, slightly overlapping.
10. Cover the inside of a pâté dish with the slices of streaky bacon.
11. Take the pan off the heat and scoop the contents in the pâté dish.
12. Push it down so that there is no air trapped inside, and fold over the overhanging slices of bacon. Cover and leave in the fridge for at least 12 hours.
13. Tip over the pâté dish, slice the balkenbrij and fry the slices in a frying pan until brown on both sides.

Serve warm with the sauerkraut.

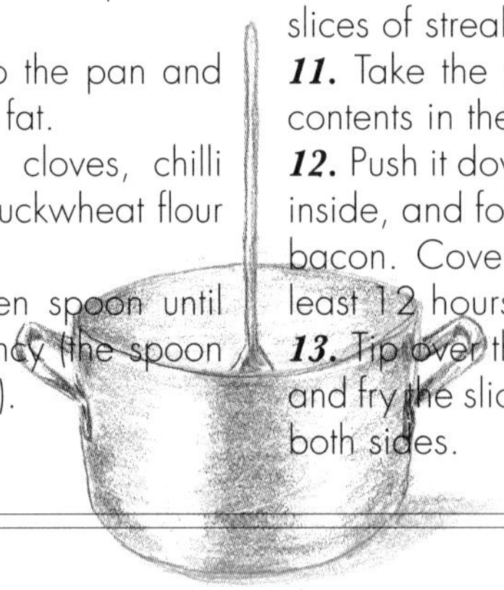

Overijssel menu

GREY PEAS WITH BACON, VINEGAR & TREACLE

400 g dried grey peas
1½ tsp salt
300 g lean smoked bacon, diced
2 tbsp apple vinegar
5 tbsp treacle
2 apples (Jonagold)
40 g butter

serves 4 – 1 night preparation – 2 hours to cook

1. Wash the grey peas and soak them overnight in a pan.
2. Add salt and boil the grey peas in the soaking liquid for 1 hour until done.
3. Wash and peel the apples and cut them in thick slices at an angle.
4. Fry the slices in the butter until brown on both sides.
5. Slowly fry the diced bacon in a frying pan on low heat.
6. Drain the grey peas and put them in a bowl. Sprinkle the vinegar and treacle over it, scoop in the fried bacon and the fat from the frying pan and stir through.
7. Spoon the grey peas on the plates and finish with the fried apple.

Overijssel menu

JAN-IN-DE-ZAK

(JACK-IN-THE-BAG)

250 g flour	*75 g raisins*
½ tsp salt	*75 g currants*
2 dl milk	*75 g dried cranberries*
150 g caster sugar	*50 g candied ginger, diced*
30 g fresh yeast	*50 g candied orange peel, diced*
seeds from 1 vanilla pod	*1 vanilla pod, emptied*
1 egg	
2 tsp cinnamon	

serves 8 – 2 hours preparation – 2 hours to cook

1. Wash and drain the currants and raisins.
2. Sift the flour over a bowl and add the salt.
3. Warm up the milk with the vanilla seeds, sugar and cinnamon until lukewarm.
4. Pour 3 tablespoons of the warm milk in a cup, add the yeast and stir until it is dissolved.
5. Make a well in the centre of the flour and pour in the milky yeast.
6. Add the egg and with a wooden spoon stir from the inside out until you have a nice dough.
7. Bit by bit, pour in the rest of the vanilla milk and give it a good stir.
8. Cover the bowl with a damp tea towel and leave to rise in a warm spot for 1 hour.
9. Then knead the raisins, currants, ginger, cranberries and orange peel through the dough.
10. Put the dough in a clean, damp and floured cotton or linen bag (if you don't have any, you could use a pillow case) and tie the top. Make sure there is enough space for the dough to rise and hang the bag in a warm spot for at least 1 hour.
11. Fill up a big pan with enough water to cover the whole bag and bring the water to the boil. Add the filled bag and boil it on low heat for about 1½ hours until done.
12. Remove the Jack-in-the-bag from the water, peel off the bag and let it dry.
13. Cut the Jack-in-the-bag into slices and serve, still warm, with a dollop of vanilla cream and red fruit.

Tips: you could also make the Jack-in-the-bag ahead. In that case, fry the slices in butter in a frying pan on high heat. Again, serve with a dollop of whipped vanilla cream and red fruit.

Or make the traditional Jack-in-the-bag: eat the slices still warm with treacle, butter and brown sugar or a scoop of vanilla ice cream, and leave out the ginger, cranberries, orange peel and fresh vanilla: these ingredients were really way too expensive!

Flevoland menu

POTATO CHEESE CROQUETTE

200 g Dutch buffalo mozzarella, cubed
200 g cheese with cloves, grated
150 g Dutch sheep's cheese, cubed
100 g mashed potato
50 g flour, sifted
50 g butter, cubed
100 ml milk
½ tsp freshly grated nutmeg
¼ tsp chilli powder
2 egg yolks
flour
200 g panko breadcrumbs
2 egg whites
1 litre sunflower or peanut oil
salt & pepper

serves 6 – 40 minutes to cook

1. Melt the butter in a sauce pan and sift the flour in. Stir well until it is well combined.
2. Add the milk and keep stirring until it is combined.
3. Now add the mashed potato, spoon by spoon, while stirring constantly.
4. Add the nutmeg, chilli powder and salt & pepper.
5. Add the mozzarella, stir until it has melted and add the sheep's cheese and then the clove cheese. If the mixture is too dry, add a little extra milk.
6. Take the pan off the heat and make a long 'sausage' of the mixture on a piece of baking paper.
7. Let it cool down and cut the sausage in pieces of 10 cm long.
8. Roll these in between your hands until they are evenly shaped.

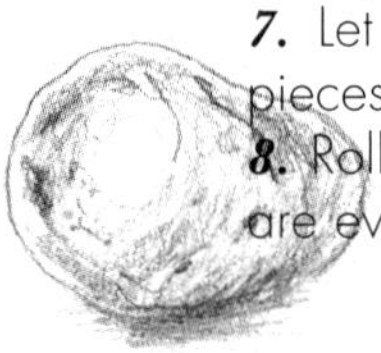

9. Roll the croquettes through the beaten egg yolks, then in the panko, then in the egg white, then in the panko, then again in the egg white and then again in the panko. Press the layers firmly onto the croquette.
10. In the meantime you have preheated the oil on the fire, until 180 °C (356 °F). Once the oil has reached that temperature, lower the heat to medium high. If you don't have a thermometer, just add a bit of panko to the oil: if it immediately starts to bubble, floats to the top and gets a colour, the temperature is right! Use a deep fry skimmer to lower the croquettes into the hot oil and to take them out. They are ready when they have turned golden brown. Drain on kitchen paper.

Lovely with sambal (Indonesian hot chilli sauce)!

DOUBT

Flevoland menu

PHEASANT WITH SAUERKRAUT & JERUSALEM ARTICHOKES

serves 6 – 1 night preparation – 1 hour and 20 minutes to cook

250 g sauerkraut (plain)
1 wine glass of cider
2 fresh bay leaves
1 clove
2 juniper berries
40 g butter, in cubes
salt & pepper

1. Warm up the sauerkraut in the cider with the butter and spices for about 20 minutes, on medium heat.
2. Stir every now and then and add salt & pepper to taste.

300 g Jerusalem artichokes
3 tbsp olive oil
1 tbsp fresh thyme, finely chopped
salt & pepper

1. Boil the Jerusalem artichokes in salted water for about 15 minutes until they are done.
2. Drain, cut the Jerusalem artichokes in pieces and mix with the olive oil, thyme, salt & pepper.
3. Put the pieces on a baking sheet and bake in a preheated oven (180 °C / 356 °F) for 15 minutes until crisp.

4 pheasant legs
1 tbsp lemon thyme, finely chopped
4 fresh bay leaves
¼ tsp chilli powder
juice and zest from 1 lemon
salt & pepper
olive oil

1. Rub the pheasant legs well with salt & pepper.
2. Place the legs in a deep oven dish and add the lemon thyme, bay leaves, lemon zest, lemon juice and chilli powder. Give it a stir and pour over the olive oil until the pheasant is just covered.
3. Wet a big piece of baking paper under the tap and use this to cover the oven dish. You could rest a couple of wooden spoons on top so that the paper won't blow off in the oven. Put the dish in the preheated oven (180 °C / 356 °F) for about 1 hour.
4. Remove the pheasant legs from the liquid and put them on a baking sheet. Put them back into the oven for about 15 minutes until crisp.

Tip: you could strain the olive oil and save it in the fridge to use again later.

Flevoland menu

CREPES WITH VANILLA ICE CREAM & ELDERFLOWER SYRUP

4 eggs	*elderflower cordial*
250 g flour	*vanilla ice cream*
1 litre full fat milk	*mint*
1 pinch of salt	*butter*

serves 6 – 25 minutes to cook

1. Sift the flour with the salt in a bowl.
2. Carefully beat in the milk, so that there are no lumps.
3. Whisk the eggs and whisk them into the batter.
4. Preheat a non-stick frying pan and when it is hot, add a small lump of butter.
5. Add a little batter (just enough to cover the bottom of the frying pan) and make sure it is evenly spread.
6. Tap the frying pan and see if the crepe comes loose. If it doesn't, add a little extra butter to the side of the pan and see if the crepe comes loose now. As soon as it does, turn it over. Fry more crepes until you have used up all the batter. Pile them onto a preheated plate and cover with another plate to keep them warm.
7. Fold the crepes into a triangular shape and pour over the elderflower cordial.
8. Garnish with a scoop of vanilla ice cream and a couple of mint leaves.
Great with elderflower lemonade (made with elderflower cordial, ice cubes and mint)!

Gelderland menu

PEARL BARLEY SOUP

100 g pearl barley
1 ½ litre water
200 g ham hock
1 tbsp salt
2 fresh bay leaves
20 g fresh ginger, sliced
100 g celeriac, cubed
1 small leek, in rings
3 onions, finely chopped
4 thin slices of smoked bacon
½ tsp freshly grated nutmeg
1 tsp chives, finely chopped
1 tsp thyme, finely chopped
salt & pepper

serves 6 – 1 night preparation – 1 ½ hours to cook

1. Wash the pearl barley, put it in a big pan, add 1 ½ litre of water, put the lid on and leave in the fridge overnight.
2. The next day, add the ham hock, salt, ginger and bay leaves and bring to the boil. Turn the heat down and boil gently for about 35 minutes.
3. Remove the ham hock, cut the meat in small pieces and return these to the pan.
4. Add the celeriac, thyme, leek and onion.
5. Bring the soup back to the boil and leave to cook gently on low heat for about 20 minutes. Give it a good stir every now and then.
6. Lay the slices of bacon in between two pieces of baking paper and put them in the preheated oven (200 °C / 392 °F) for about 7 minutes, until crisp.
7. Season the pearl barley soup with chives, nutmeg and pepper, divide it over the plates and finish each plate with a slice of bacon.

Gelderland menu

STOCKFISH WITH ENDIVE

800 g stockfish	*1 kg potatoes*
2 fresh bay leaves	*3 dl milk*
2 dl milk	*500 g endive*
20 g butter	*1 pinch of salt*
1 dl water	*30 g butter*
	½ tsp freshly grated nutmeg
	½ dl cooking liquid from the stockfish
	1 dl milk
	75 g butter at room temperature, cubed

serves 6 – 24 hours preparation – 40 minutes to cook

1. Soak the stockfish overnight in a generous amount of water in the fridge. Rinse it well after soaking!
2. Remove the skin and fish bones.
3. Bring the fish to the boil with the milk, butter, bay leaves and water, turn the heat down and boil it gently for 40 minutes.
4. When the fish is done (it looks opaque) lift it from the cooking liquid. Keep the liquid.

In the meantime, prepare the endive.
1. Boil the potatoes for 20 minutes in water until they are done. Take care not to add too much water because that makes the potatoes too moist.
2. While the potatoes are boiling, wash the endive and chop it. Drain it well.
3. Put the milk in a sauce pan and warm it up but don't let it boil.
4. When the potatoes are done, take them off the heat and drain them.
5. Put the potatoes back into the pan, add the butter and pour over the warm milk.
6. Mash it well until you have a creamy mash.
7. Now add the stockfish, some of its cooking liquid, milk and the endive. Season to taste with pepper, nutmeg and salt, if needed. This is a very salty dish because of the stockfish, so be careful with the salt and keep on tasting while making it.

Gelderland menu

ARNHEMSE MEISJES

(ARNHEM BISCUITS)

200 g flour
20 g lemon zest
25 g granulated sugar
7 g fresh yeast
1¼ dl milk
5 g salt
150 g butter at room temperature, in cubes
250 g cane sugar

serves 8 – 30 minutes preparation – 25 minutes oven – 20 minutes to cook

1. Mix 20 g lemon zest and 25 g granulated sugar together. This is lemon sugar.
2. On your worktop, put down the flour in a circular shape and make a well in the centre.
3. Add the lemon sugar, yeast, milk and salt to the well. Carefully mix this with your fingers until you have a consistent dough.
4. Now add the butter and keep kneading the dough until the butter is mixed in well.
5. Shape the dough into a rectangle of roughly 1 cm thick, cover this and let the dough harden in the fridge for 15 minutes.
6. Cut the dough in squares of roughly 1½ x 1½ cm; roll these into small balls and put them back into the fridge for about 10 minutes to harden (watch out that the dough doesn't get too hard).
7. Dust the worktop with cane sugar and put the dough balls on top.
8. Roll the balls in the sugar and press them flat until 3 mm thick.
9. Put the cookies on a baking sheet covered with baking paper and bake them in a preheated oven (155 °C / 311 °F) for 25 minutes.
10. Take the cookies off the baking sheet and let them cool down on a cooling rack.

Delicious with a cup of tea or coffee!

Utrecht menu

CHERVIL SOUP & HETE BLIKSEM
(MASHED APPLES AND POTATOES)

CHERVIL SOUP

1 calf's trotter
300 g veal knuckle
1 litre water
2 fresh bay leaves
½ chilli, deseeded
2 onions, finely chopped
3 tbsp olive oil
10 g fine dry breadcrumbs
1 egg yolk
salt & pepper
1 tsp freshly grated nutmeg
2 bunches of chervil, washed and cut (keep half a bunch for garnish)
2 leeks, washed and sliced
½ litre cooking cream

serves 6 — 2 hours and 15 minutes preparation — 40 minutes to cook

1. Put the trotter, veal knuckle, olive oil, bay leaves, chilli and onions on the heat in a high pan and briefly brown the outsides while stirring. Ask your butcher to cut the trotter for you.
2. Now add 1 litre of water, bring to the boil, turn the heat down and boil gently for 2 hours.
3. Remove the trotter and the veal knuckle from the pan, pull the meat off the bone and mince it. Put the mince in a bowl.
4. Add the leek and chervil (save half a bunch for garnish) to the stock in the pan and leave to boil briskly for about 20 minutes.
5. Now add the nutmeg, salt & pepper, egg yolk and the crumbs with the minced meat in the bowl, mix it all through and shape the mixture into small meat balls.
6. Remove the bay leaves and use a handheld blender to puree the soup.
7. Now add the meat balls and cream. Bring the soup back to the boil and let it boil gently for about 15 minutes.
8. Season to taste with salt & pepper and garnish the soup with the left over chervil.

HETE BLIKSEM (MASHED APPLES AND POTATOES)

500 g lean smoked bacon
1 fresh bay leaf
2 juniper berries
5 dl water
1 kg potatoes
500 g cooking apples
500 g dessert apples
50 g butter, cubed
1 smoked sausage
salt & pepper

serves 6 — 1 hour and 40 minutes to cook

1. Put the bacon, bay leaf and juniper berries in a big cast iron pan, add 5 dl water and bring to the boil.
2. Turn down the heat and let it boil gently for about 30 minutes.
3. In the meantime, peel the potatoes and apples, core the apples, and cut them all in pieces. Add these to the bacon and water; it should be just covered. Bring to the boil, turn the heat down and let it boil for about 30 minutes.
4. In the meantime, warm up the smoked sausage for 15 minutes in hot, not boiling, water.
5. After 30 minutes, remove the bacon from the pan and mash the potatoes and apples with the butter on a low heat. Season to taste with salt & pepper. Cut the bacon and smoked sausage into slices and put the meat on top of the mashed apples and potatoes.

Utrecht menu

SEMOLINA PUDDING

1 litre milk	*Tip:*
1 pinch of salt	*4 figs*
60 g semolina	*½ vanilla pod*
40 g sugar	*juice of 1 orange*
½ vanilla pod, emptied	*peel of 1 orange*
30 g candied ginger	*1 glass of red wine*
3 leaves of gelatine	*30 g sugar*

serves 4 – 20 minutes to cook – 30 minutes to cool

1. *Tip: put the red wine with the sugar, vanilla pod (also the empty other half), orange juice and peel in a sauce pan on low heat and let it reduce until you have a syrup (about 20 minutes).*

2. In the meantime, bring the milk with the emptied seeds from the other half of the vanilla pod and the salt to the boil.

3. Mix the semolina, sugar and candied ginger and add it to the boiling milk while stirring well. Let this boil gently for about 10 minutes, while stirring all the time.

4. In the meantime, soak the gelatine in water and then dissolve the gelatine leaves in 3 tablespoons of the warm milk. Make sure there are no lumps.

5. Whisk this thoroughly through the semolina pudding and then tip the contents of the pan into a jelly mould, rinsed with cold water.

6. Let the semolina cool down and put it in the fridge for at least 30 minutes.

Tip: in the meantime, slice the figs.

7. Place the outside of the mould in warm water (watch out that no water spills onto the pudding), lay a plate on top and turn the mould and plate over together.

Tip: arrange the figs around the pudding and pour the syrup over the semolina and figs.

Noord-Holland menu

VEGETABLE SOUP WITH MEATBALLS

serves 6 – 4 hours and 30 minutes preparation – 30 minutes to cook

100 g minced meat, half pork, half beef
1 tbsp fine breadcrumbs
salt & pepper
½ tsp freshly grated nutmeg
1 tsp smooth mustard
1 tsp Indonesian soy sauce (kecap)

1. Put the minced meat, breadcrumbs, salt & pepper, nutmeg, mustard and kecap in a bowl and mix it well with your hands.

2. Pick off small bits and in between your hand palms shape the meat into small meatballs of about 1 cm.

500 g beef shin
200 g marrowbone
2 litre water
2 cloves
½ chilli
100 g onions, chopped
50 g leek, chopped
100 g carrot, quartered
1 bulb of fennel, chopped
stems of ½ bunch of flat leaf parsley
2 fresh bay leaves
1 mace
½ bunch of lovage, stems and leaves
2 stems of celery, sliced
50 g celeriac, cubed
50 g leek, sliced
50 g cauliflower, in small florets
50 g fennel, finely chopped
50 g red pepper, cubed
3 tbsp flat leaf parsley, finely chopped
50 g vermicelli

1. Put the shin and marrowbone in a big pan with 1 teaspoon of salt and cover with 2 litres of water.
2. Bring slowly to the boil. Scoop the foam off with a spoon. Now add cloves, chilli, bay, carrot, leek, fennel, mace and the stems of flat leaf parsley.
3. Leave this to stew on very low heat for about 4 hours. The stock should only ripple slightly and definitely shouldn't boil!
4. Cover a sieve with a piece of cheese cloth, put it on a big pan and strain the stock. Take the meat off the bone. Keep the meat and the bone for later.
5. Let the stock cool down and carefully skim off the fat that floats on top.
6. Now put the stock back onto the heat and bring to the boil again.
7. Add all the vegetables, except the leek and parsley. Leave to boil gently, covered and on low heat, for about 10 minutes.
8. Now add the leek, parsley and meatballs. After 5 minutes, also add the vermicelli.
9. Leave to boil gently for another 10 minutes and add salt & pepper to taste.
10. Now add the meat from the bone and marrowbone.
11. Remove the marrowbone from the soup and spread the contents over white toasted bread.

Noord-Holland menu

POTATO AND CHICORY GRATIN WITH HAM & CHEESE SAUCE

1 kg floury potatoes
100 g butter
3 dl milk
½ tsp freshly grated nutmeg
8 small heads of chicory
250 g ham off the bone, in thin slices
250 g boiled and smoked streaky bacon, in thin slices
60 g butter
50 g flour
225 g old Gouda cheese, grated
5 dl milk
salt & pepper

serves 6 – 30 minutes to cook – 20 minutes in the oven

1. Boil the potatoes until they are done.
2. Now mash the potatoes with 3 dl milk.
3. Add the butter and season to taste with salt, pepper and nutmeg.
4. Spread the mashed potato evenly over the bottom of an oven dish and cover with the boiled and smoked streaky bacon.
5. Now make the cheese sauce. Warm up 5 dl milk with 60 g butter and add the flour bit by bit.
6. When the sauce has puffed for at least three times, add most of the grated cheese and stir well. Wait until the cheese has melted completely and then season to taste with salt, pepper and nutmeg.
7. Save the rest of the grated cheese to garnish the dish.
8. Wash the chicory and half the heads lengthwise; remove the hard, bitter core.
9. Cover the bacon with the chicory halves.
10. Add the slices of ham and pour the cheese sauce over.
11. Sprinkle the rest of the grated cheese over and put the dish in a preheated oven (180 °C / 356 °F) for about 20 minutes.

Noord-Holland menu

APPLE PIE

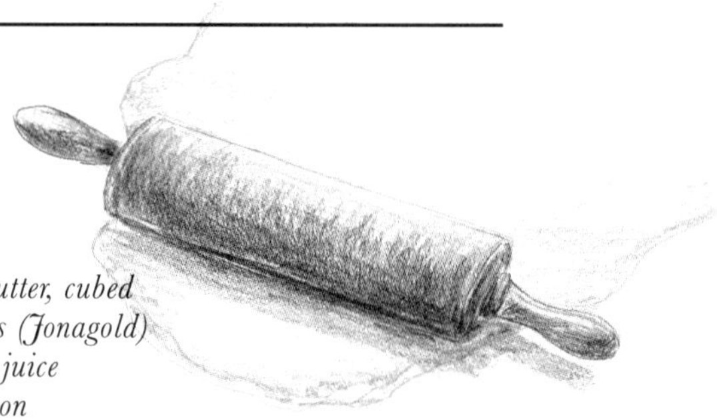

100 g raisins	*200 g cold butter, cubed*
50 g currants	*1½ kg apples (Jonagold)*
100 g dried cranberries	*1 tbsp lemon juice*
100 g dried apricots	*zest of 1 lemon*
350 g self-raising flour	*5 tsp cinnamon*
1 pinch of salt	*2 tbsp apricot jam*
3 eggs	*2 slices sponge loaf*
250 g golden caster sugar	*2 tbsp ground almonds*

serves 12 – 1 hour and 25 minutes preparation – 70 minutes in the oven – 20 minutes to cook

1. Soak the raisins, currants, cranberries and apricots in lukewarm water for at least 1 hour.

2. Sift the self-raising flour into a big bowl and add salt and lemon zest.

3. Beat the eggs (save 1 beaten egg to finish the pie with), add them to the flour and mix well.

4. Stir and then knead the dough, and add 175 g caster sugar and butter while you do so. Knead the dough until it isn't sticky anymore and it shapes into a ball. Wrap the dough ball in cling film and leave in the fridge for at least 15 minutes.

5. In the meantime, peel the apples and cut into small pieces (you can also use other varieties, like Bramley) and drain the dried fruits. Mix the apple with the dried fruit, 75 g caster sugar, lemon juice and cinnamon. The longer you leave this to rest, the better the taste will be!

6. Grease a spring form cake tin with butter. Usually, I also cover the bottom with baking paper. Now take the dough from the fridge and knead it again.

7. Dust the worktop with flour and roll out the dough until it is about ½ cm thick. Cover the spring form cake tin with the dough – first the bottom, then the sides. Make sure the dough hangs over the edges so that you can cut it off neatly along the rim (note: do this only after you have added the filling). Keep some dough to cover the cake with.

8. Crumble the slices of sponge loaf and sprinkle them over the bottom. Then add the ground almonds.

9. Now add the apple mixture and push this right down.

10. Shape the left over dough into long, thin strips and lay these down criss-cross on top of the apple filling. Brush the dough with 1 beaten egg.

11. Bake the apple pie in the middle of a preheated oven (175 °C / 347 °F) for about 70 minutes.

12. Warm up the apricot jam with 2 tablespoons of water until it is liquid and brush this over the top of the apple pie as soon as it comes out of the oven. Leave to cool in the tin for at least 15 minutes and then undo the springform. After about 45 minutes the apple pie is ready to serve.

Nice with whipped cream!

Zuid-Holland menu

HERRING SALAD & HUTSPOT (MASH) FROM LEIDEN

HERRING SALAD

4 raw herrings
2 beetroots, boiled
2 tbsp dill, finely chopped
1 tbsp yogurt
1 tbsp mayonnaise
2 tbsp jenever (Dutch gin)
4 slices of rye bread
juice and zest of 1 orange
salt & pepper

serves 4 – 15 minutes to cook

1. Cut the herring and beetroot into small cubes.
2. Mix the yogurt with mayonnaise, gin, and the juice and zest of the orange.
3. Season to taste with salt & pepper and mix in the dill.
4. Now add the beetroot and herring to the dressing.
5. Garnish the salad with some dill.
6. Nice with a couple of slices of dark rye bread and a small glass of jenever. *Proost! (Cheers!)*

MASH FROM LEIDEN

300 g dried white beans
300 g lean smoked bacon, diced
750 g carrots, peeled and cut into pieces
500 g parsnips, peeled and cut into pieces
300 g onions, in rings
15 g salt
60 g butter, cubed
250 g cheese with cumin, grated
1 smoked sausage
salt & pepper

serves 6 – 1 night preparation – 40 minutes to cook

1. Wash the beans and soak them overnight, in plenty water, covered, in the fridge.
2. Boil the beans in the soaking liquid, together with the diced bacon. Bring to the boil, turn the heat down and let it boil gently for about 20 minutes.
3. Now add the carrot, parsnip, onion rings and salt to the beans and cook gently for about 40 minutes.
4. Warm up the smoked sausage in warm (but not boiling) water for 15 minutes and slice it.
5. Drain the vegetables, add the butter and cumin cheese (save 100 grams for garnish) and mash it all well. Season to taste with pepper and, if needed, salt; but it is probably already quite salty because of the bacon.
6. Put down the slices of smoked sausage on top of the mash and finish with the rest of the cumin cheese.

Zuid-Holland menu

HAAGSE BLUF

(WHIPPED EGG WHITES IN REDCURRANT SAUCE)

350 g redcurrants	*150 g raspberries*
½ dl water	*150 g redcurrants*
1 star anise	*2 egg whites*
1 tbsp caster sugar	*60 g caster sugar*
200 g strawberries	*1 tbsp mint leaves, shredded*

serves 6 – 35 minutes to cook

1. Gently pull 350 g redcurrants off the stems, put them in a sauce pan and add the water, star anise and sugar.
2. Put the lid on, bring to the boil, lower the heat and boil gently for about 15 minutes.
3. Put a sieve on a bowl and strain the redcurrants. With the back of a spoon, press out all the juice.
4. Clean the strawberries, raspberries and 150 g redcurrants and divide them over the plates with the redcurrant sauce.
5. Now beat the egg whites with the sugar until you have an airy foam. You could also add some redcurrant juice which makes the foam pink!
6. With one or two tablespoons, shape the foam into ovals and put these on the plates.
7. Take your kitchen blow torch and use it to brown the top of the foam. (Don't worry if you don't have a blow torch – just leave the foam as it is.) This is a nice dessert to serve in glasses or ice cream glass. Note: you only whip the egg white just before serving! The rest of the Haagse bluf can be prepared in advance.

Zeeland menu

LUKEWARM SALAD WITH SEA ASTER, SAMPHIRE AND BASIL WITH LOBSTER & GRAPEFRUIT

1 lobster	*1 grapefruit*
2 tbsp sea salt	*½ chilli, finely chopped*
1 tbsp fennel seeds	*1 tbsp white wine vinegar*
1 bunch of basil	*3 tbsp sunflower oil*
200 g sea aster	*salt & pepper*
200 g samphire	*some butter*

serves 4 – 20 minutes to cook

1. Bring a big pan of water to the boil with sea salt, the stems of the basil and the fennel seeds.
2. As soon as the water boils, add the living lobster. Boil for 7 minutes, take it out and let it cool down.
3. As soon as the lobster is cool enough to handle, remove the meat from the shell. (If you wait until the lobster has cooled down completely, it is much harder to remove the meat!)
4. Peel the grapefruit and cut the segments out from in between the membrane.
5. Squeeze the juice from the membrane in a bowl and add the white wine vinegar, chilli, pepper & salt. Add the sunflower and olive oil, drop by drop, while you whisk. This is the dressing.
6. Blanch the sea aster and samphire briefly in boiling water and then gently fry them for 3 minutes in a sauce pan with some butter and basil (save some basil leaves to garnish the salad with). Add some ground pepper.
7. Divide the vegetables over the plates and add the grapefruit, basil leaves and the lobster. Finish with the dressing.

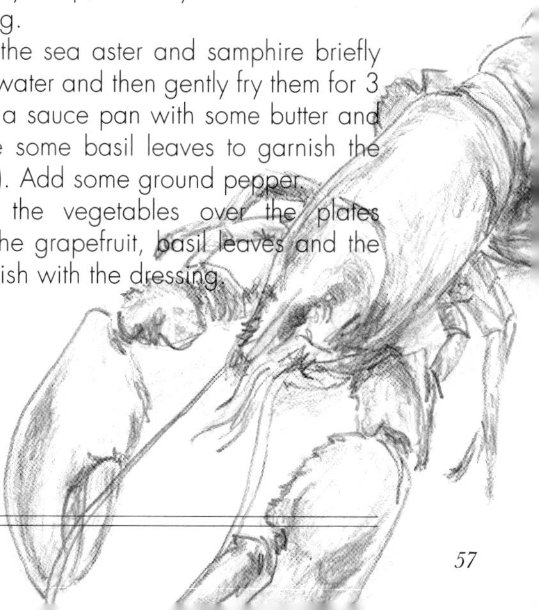

Zeeland menu

MUSSELS

2 kg mussels
1 dl dry white wine
3 big onions
1 leek
1 big carrot
5 stems of celery
½ bunch of flat leaf parsley
½ bunch of leaf celery
½ chilli
1 tbsp white wine vinegar
1 tbsp thyme
olive oil
salt & pepper

serves 4 – 15 minutes preparation – 10 minutes to cook

1. Wash the mussels. (If there are any mussels open, close them. If they stay closed, you can use them.)
2. Remove any mussels that are damaged or still open.
3. Pull off the beards.
4. Put a big pan on high heat, add 2 tablespoons of olive oil, add the onions, celery, chilli, carrot and leek and fry these until the onions are translucent.
5. Now add the mussels and stir through.
6. Pour in the white wine and white wine vinegar, and add the thyme, parsley and leaf celery.
7. Stir again until all the mussels will have been in contact with the hot bottom of the pan.
8. When all the mussels have opened, they are done.

Great with some bread and dips.

Zeeland menu

ZEEUWSE BOLUSSEN

(CINNAMON ROLLS)

400 g flour	*200 g butter*
1 pinch of salt	*1 egg*
4½ dl milk	*250 g brown caster sugar*
3 tsp vanilla aroma	*2 tsp cinnamon*
50 g fresh yeast	

serves 8 – 1 hour and 30 minutes to prepare – 20 minutes in the oven – 20 minutes to rise

1. Sift the flour into a bowl and add the salt.
2. Warm up the milk until it is lukewarm and pour out 2 dl. Dissolve and melt the yeast and butter in this 2 dl warm milk.
3. Now add the vanilla aroma to the 2½ dl lukewarm milk and stir well.
4. Make a well in the flour and pour in the milk-yeast mixture.
5. Beat the egg and add this to the well too.
6. Start kneading from the inside out and little by little add the lukewarm vanilla milk.
7. Keep kneading until you have an elastic dough. Cover the bowl with a damp tea towel and leave to rest for 1 hour.
8. In the meantime, mix the brown sugar with the cinnamon.
9. After the dough has risen, knead it again.
10. Now dust the worktop with flour and roll out the dough until you have a rectangle of roughly 2 cm thick.
11. Sprinkle the cinnamon sugar mixture over the dough and roll it up.
12. Now cut the roll in slices of about 2 cm thick. These are the bolussen.
13. Put the bolussen on a greased baking sheet (or a baking sheet covered with baking paper) and leave to rise for 20 minutes.
14. Put the baking sheet in a preheated oven (225 °C / 437 °F) for 20 minutes.
15. Take the bolussen out of the oven and let them cool down on a wire rack, so that the air can get to them. Lovely to eat lukewarm with a scoop of vanilla ice cream.

Brabant menu

SAUSAGE ROLL

250 g flour	*½ tsp nutmeg*
1 pinch of salt	*¼ tsp cinnamon*
1½ dl milk	*¼ tsp chilli powder*
20 g fresh yeast	*1 tbsp Indonesian soy sauce (kecap)*
50 g butter	*2 eggs*
250 g lean pork mince	*40 g dry, fine breadcrumbs*
salt & pepper	

serves 6 – 1 hour and 30 minutes preparation – 30 minutes to cook – 30 minutes in the oven

1. Warm up the milk until it is lukewarm and add the yeast.
2. Sift the flour and salt into a bowl.
3. Melt the butter in a small sauce pan and let it cool down. Make a well in the flour and pour in the milk-yeast mixture and the melted butter.
4. Knead it until you have a smooth dough. If the dough is still wet and sticky, add some more flour until you have a nice big, smooth dough ball. Leave the dough to rise (covered with a damp tea towel) on a warm spot for about 1 hour.
5. Season the mince with the nutmeg, kecap, chilli powder, cinnamon and salt & pepper.
6. Now add the 2 eggs (keep a little bit of egg to the side for later) and the fine breadcrumbs and mix everything well.
7. Dust your worktop with flour and roll out the dough until it is roughly ½ cm thick.
8. Cut the dough in rectangles of 8 x 10 cm and spoon some of the mince on one side of each rectangle.
9. Fold the dough over the mince, press the opening closed with your fingers and shape it into a wave while doing so.
10. Put the rolls onto a baking sheet covered in baking paper and leave to rest for at least 15 minutes.
11. Put the rolls in a preheated oven (180 °C / 356 °F) for 30 minutes or until they are golden brown. *The sausage rolls are best when still warm!*

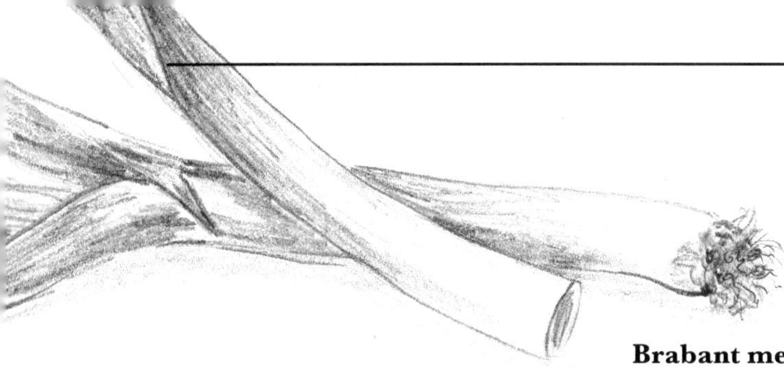

Brabant menu

PREIPROL

(POTATO LEEK SOUP)

2 litres of vegetable stock
(bring 3 onions, 1 leek, 1 big carrot, 1 bay leaf, 1 celeriac, 1 stalk of celery, 1 clove of garlic with salt & pepper to the boil in 4 litres of water and leave this to boil gently for 1½ hours, then drain)

75 g rice
4 potatoes
500 g leek
1 smoked sausage
100 g raw beef fat
salt & pepper

serves 6 – 2 hours preparation – 30 minutes to cook

1. Bring the stock to the boil in a big pan.
2. Wash the rice, peel the potatoes and cut them into pieces.
3. Wash the leeks and slice them.
4. Stir the rice and leek through the stock and let boil.
5. After 10 minutes boiling add the potatoes and let boil for another 20 minutes.
6. Warm up the smoked sausage in hot, not boiling, water for 15 minutes and then slice the sausage.
7. Cut the beef fat into cubes and fry them in a frying pan on low heat until they release the fat (what you have left is in Dutch called 'kaantjes').
8. Season the soup to taste with salt & pepper.
9. Serve the soup in bowls and finish with the slices of smoked sausage and the kaantjes.

Brabant menu

BOSSCHE BOLLEN

(CHOCOLATE PROFITEROLES)

1 dl water
40 g butter
½ tsp salt
50 g flour
2 eggs
2½ dl whipping cream
2 tbsp icing sugar
seeds from ½ vanilla pod
1 egg white

100 g icing sugar
2 tbsp cocoa powder
1 egg white

serves 6 – 20 minutes in the oven – 30 minutes to cook

1. Put the water, butter and salt in a pan with heavy bottom and bring to the boil.
2. Sift the flour over a bowl and add this all at the same time to the boiling water while stirring constantly.
3. Keep stirring until a dough ball forms in the pan.
4. Take the pan off the heat and add the eggs one at a time. Add the second egg when the first one has been incorporated into the dough. Keep stirring until you have a nice shiny dough.
5. Divide the dough into 6 balls and lay these on a buttered baking sheet. Put the profiteroles in a preheated oven (225 °C / 437 °F) for 20 minutes until they are done and have turned golden brown.
6. Turn the oven off, open the oven door just a little and leave the profiteroles to cool down inside the oven for 10 minutes.
7. In the meantime, whip the cream with the icing sugar, vanilla seeds and the egg white until stiff.
8. Sift the 100 grams of icing sugar with the cocoa powder over a bowl. Stir in the other egg white, a drop a time, until you have a thick, shiny mixture.
9. Fill a piping bag with the whipped cream and use it to fill the Bossche bollen, by making a little hole underneath, through which you can stick the piping bag.
10. Brush the tops with the cocoa icing.

ASPARAGUS WITH POACHED EGGS & HOLLANDAISE SAUCE

500 g white asparagus
salt
2 mace
2 tbsp olive oil

6 eggs
1 tbsp white wine vinegar
4 egg yolks

4 tbsp white wine vinegar
½ tbsp freshly ground pepper
1 banana shallot, halved
1 pinch of salt
2 stems of tarragon
150 g butter, cubed
Maldon sea salt

serves 6 – 35 minutes to cook

1. Peel the asparagus with a potato peeler and cut off the hard ends. Start peeling 1 cm under the 'head' of the asparagus. Make sure you peel them all the way around because the outsides are not easy to eat. But also be careful not to cut away too much… *Tip: save the peels and ends to make asparagus soup with later.*
2. Bring a wide pan of water to the boil with salt and mace. Lower the asparagus into the boiling water and cover them with a wet tea towel. This will push the asparagus down into the water.
3. Bring the water back to the boil and leave to boil gently for 10 minutes. If by then the asparagus are not completely done, leave them in the cooking liquid for a little longer. *Tip: you could use this cooking liquid for asparagus soup.* Cut the asparagus into smaller pieces and season to taste with a little olive oil, pepper & salt.
4. Pour 4 tbsp of white wine vinegar in a small sauce pan with the pepper, salt, shallot and tarragon and let this boil for 10 minutes.
5. Strain the liquid, put it in a bowl and place this on top of a sauce pan with boiling water.
6. Whisk in the egg yokes plus the butter cubes until you have a silky smooth sauce. Be careful that the sauce doesn't get too hot, or you will end up with scrambled egg. As soon as you take it off the heat, it will cool down and thicken. This is the hollandaise sauce.
7. In the meantime, bring a sauce pan with water and a splash of white wine vinegar to the boil. Turn down the heat: it is important that the water doesn't boil anymore, it should be just under boiling point.
8. Stir the water so that you get a whirlpool and then break the eggs into the water one at a time. Make sure they don't touch. Leave the eggs in the water for about 3 minutes. Usually they will float to the top when the egg whites are set.
9. Slice some tarragon for garnish.
10. Spoon some hollandaise sauce on each plate and divide the asparagus on top.
11. Lay the poached eggs on top of the asparagus and finish with Maldon sea salt, freshly ground pepper and the tarragon.

Limburg menu

SOUR MEAT

1 kg lean braising steak	*4 onions, in half rings*
2 dl white wine vinegar	*100 g butter*
1½ tsp salt	*2 tbsp olive oil*
½ tsp freshly ground pepper	*1 tbsp treacle*
3 fresh bay leaves	*2 tbsp apple syrup*
3 cloves	*6 slices of gingerbread loaf, cubed*
4 juniper berries	*1 tbsp blackcurrant jam*
3 tbsp thyme, finely chopped	

serves 4 – 8 hours preparation – 2 hours and 30 minutes to cook

1. Dice the meat and rub well with salt & pepper.
2. Put the pieces in a bowl with the vinegar, bay leaves, cloves, juniper berries and thyme. Stir well.
3. Cover the bowl well and leave to marinate in the fridge for at least 8 hours. After that, remove the meat from the marinade and dry it (keep the marinade).
4. Melt 60 grams of butter with the olive oil in a big, heavy frying pan and brown the meat.
5. In a separate frying pan, fry the onions in 40 grams of butter until translucent, then add them to the meat.
6. Stir well, add the treacle, gingerbread loaf cubes and the marinade. Give it another stir.
7. Put the lid on the pan and leave it all to stew on low heat for at least 2 hours. Every now and then, check to see if the meat doesn't stick to the bottom of the pan.
8. Finally, stir in the blackcurrant jam and then serve with boiled potatoes and sauerkraut.

Limburg menu

PLUM FLAN

800 g plums	*175 g golden caster sugar*
3 star anise	*150 g butter, cubed, on room temperature*
4 cardamom pods	*3 tbsp milk*
3 tbsp raw cane sugar	*1 egg*
375 g flour	*1 vanilla pod*
1½ tsp baking powder	*100 g ground almonds*
1 pinch of salt	

serves 12 – 1 night preparation – 40 minutes to cook – 25 minutes in the oven

1. Wash the plums and soak them in water with star anise, vanilla seeds and the pod, cane sugar and cardamom seeds. Cover the bowl and put in the fridge overnight.
2. The next day, you make the dough. First, sift the flour, baking powder, salt and caster sugar in a bowl.
3. Then add the butter cubes, milk and egg.
4. Knead this all together until you have a smooth dough. Shape it into a ball, cover it and leave to rest in the fridge for at least 1 hour.
5. In the meantime, remove the stones from the plums and bring the plums to the boil in the soaking liquid. Let them boil gently for 10 minutes. Take out 12 plums, slice them and keep the slices separate.
6. Drain the plums and puree them in a food processor.
7. Take the dough from the fridge, flour the worktop and roll out the dough until it is big enough to cover the bottom and sides of the tart tin.
8. Grease the tart tin and cover bottom and sides with the dough. Every bit that hangs over, you can cut away along the rim.
9. Cover the dough with baking paper, fill this with baking beans and put the tin in the preheated oven (200 °C / 392 °F) for 20 minutes.
10. Take the tin out of the oven, remove the baking paper and beans and cover the bottom with the ground almonds. Spoon in the plum puree and finish with a circle of the slices of plums that you kept behind.
11. Put the tart tin back into the hot oven (200 °C / 392 °F) for 25 minutes until done.

Becht Lifestyle

English translation: Roselle de Jong
Photography: Rene Mesman
Styling: Hanna van den Bos
Design & illustrations: Studio Ultradeluxe, Fleur van Maarschalkerwaart
Lithography: Marc Gijzen

ISBN 978 90 230 1431 7
NUR 440

www.becht-boeken.nl